My Daddy Forgets
There is a Boo-Boo in his Head

Written By: Captain Brad Blazek
Illustrated By: TullipStudio

Copyright © 2021 Brad Blazek

All rights reserved. No part of this publication may be reproduced, distributed, or transmitted in any form or by any means, including photocopying, recording, or other electronic or mechanical methods, without the prior written permission of the publisher, except in the case of brief quotations embodied in critical reviews and certain other noncommercial uses permitted by copyright law.

This is a work of fiction. Any similarities to any real persons, living or deceased, are purely coincidental and not intended by the author.

ISBN 978-1-7371591-1-7

It can be difficult for young children to understand their parent having a disability. They may have many questions like why they have to be more quiet than other kids, why their parent can't play with them like they see other parents do with other kids, or why their mommy or daddy gets upset or stressed so quickly or easily.

This book is told from the perspective of a young child (a big sister) as she explains life in their family to her baby sister. This book shows what it is like for young children living with their daddy who has a brain injury. This is a story of love, empathy, understanding, struggle and triumph.

Special thanks to my loving wife (and caregiver) Terri, for always supporting me and helping me pursue my dreams.

To my beautiful daughters Belle and Snow for showing me different ways to do things and helping me remember.

To the Writer's Guild Initiative and Fred Graver for all your help in fine tuning my story.

To you, the reader, for helping me tell the story.

Daddy has a boo-boo in his head.

His head hurts every day.

He was an Army Soldier.

He got hurt when he was fighting the bad guys in war to keep us all safe, and to keep our country safe.

Daddy is our hero.

Mommy says that Daddy is okay, but he needs extra help to do things,

and we can help Daddy.

She is his caregiver.

Mommy is like a nurse to Daddy.

I know Daddy loves us because he tells us.

Sometimes he acts confused or forgets where he is or what he was doing.

But even when he forgets to show it, I know Daddy loves us.

Daddy needs a stick to help him walk.

It is called a cane.

Sometimes Daddy forgets he needs it...

Sometimes Daddy falls,

I help him...

I am a big helper...

You can be too.

Daddy has trouble getting up.

I like being up in the morning with the sun.

His boo-boo hurts in the morning.

We have to be quiet, but I want to play.

I try my best and Mommy helps.

I help Daddy to wake up with a kiss and hug.

You can help Daddy too.

Mommy can take us to go outside and play, so we can play loud.

Daddy loves us
and tries to cook, he really does try...
It is fun because I never know what he will cook...
Mommy has to help Daddy... A LOT !!! hehe

It is fun to go places with Daddy. Every time we go anywhere it is an adventure. Sometimes he forgets where we are going, I help him remember, and you can help him remember too.

It is fun to be silly with Daddy.
You can be silly with Daddy too!

We can help him by being a little quiet.
Sometimes, when Daddy is playing with us, it is fun, and we get loud. The loud sounds make Daddy's boo-boo hurt, and he covers his ears.

Or when we're in the car and we sing loud. It's fun to sing, and Daddy wants us to sing. And he sings too but Daddy forgets it hurts his boo-boo and then his head hurts.
Mommy and I tell Daddy that the singing has to be soft.
Shhh...
Daddy and Mommy tell me they want us to be happy and make happy sounds.
It helps if we all remember there's a boo-boo in Daddy's head.

We help Daddy remember he has headphones for the happy noises. He puts on his headphones. Sometimes he goes outside. He can see us through the window while we sing and dance.

I am a big helper. And one day little sister you will be able to help him too. Daddy says I help him to remember...

I help him remember how good a hug can feel.
I help him remember how sweet a laugh sounds.

I help him remember love. You do too.
Daddy loves us,
but sometimes Daddy forgets.

When he remembers, he tells my sister and me:
"That's right sweet ones, when I held you after you were born...
You were so small and so full of love.
You taught me how good love can feel.
You both did."
Thank you for being my sweet girls, I love you!"

The End

About the Author

Captain Brad Blazek is medically retired from the United States Army for wounds received in combat in Iraq.

He holds a masters degree in Clinical Mental Health Counseling and is completing a doctorate in Clinical Psychology. He has volunteered his time helping other Soldiers, Veterans, family members and those with low-income in the community, over the last 12 years.

He has been awarded the LPCA Humanitarian of the Year 2019 for the State of Georgia, Presidential Letter of commendation from the President of the United States of America, and many medals from the Military including the Purple Heart, Bronze Star, Meritorious Service Medal, Army Commendation Medal, Commander's Service Medal for volunteering, among many others. He has a wife as his caregiver and two daughters.

He believes in trying every little thing life has to offer. He has flown airplanes, driven a tank, operated heavy earth moving construction equipment, become a master scuba diver, ridden horses, ridden motorcycles, and wants every child to follow their dreams and make new ones as they grow. "Do not let disabilities hold you back from dreaming big and shooting for the Stars."

Made in the USA
Las Vegas, NV
01 June 2024